Red Dragonfly
on My
Shoulder

RED DRAGONFLY ON MY SHOULDER

Haiku translated by Sylvia Cassedy and Kunihiro Suetake

Illustrated by Molly Bang

HarperCollins*Publishers*

Red Dragonfly on My Shoulder   Text copyright © 1992 by the estate of Sylvia Cassedy and Kunihiro Suetake   Illustrations copyright © 1992 by Molly Bang   Printed in the U.S.A. All rights reserved. 1 2 3 4 5 6 7 8 9 10 First Edition   Library of Congress Cataloging-in-Publication Data   Red dragonfly on my shoulder : haiku / translated by Sylvia Cassedy and Kunihiro Suetake ; illustrated by Molly Bang.   p.   cm.   Translated from the Japanese.   Summary: Thirteen haiku about animals, translated from the Japanese and illustrated with collages and assemblages.   ISBN 0-06-022624-2. — ISBN 0-06-022625-0 (lib. bdg.)   1. Haiku—Translations into English.   2. Animals—Poetry.   I. Cassedy, Sylvia.   II. Suetake, Kunihiro, date.   III. Bang, Molly, ill.   PL782.E3R4   1992   895.6'1008—dc20   91-18443   CIP   AC

R0093652985

Red Dragonfly
on My
Shoulder

Red dragonfly on my shoulder calls me his friend. Autumn has arrived.

Sōseki

Leaping flying fish! Dancing for me and my boat as I sail for home.

Kôson

Detestable crow! Today alone you please me—black against the snow.

Bashô

Galloping pony—alone, against the moonlight, on a whitened beach.

Kyorai!

Little frog among rain-shaken leaves, are you, too, splashed with fresh, green paint?

Gaki

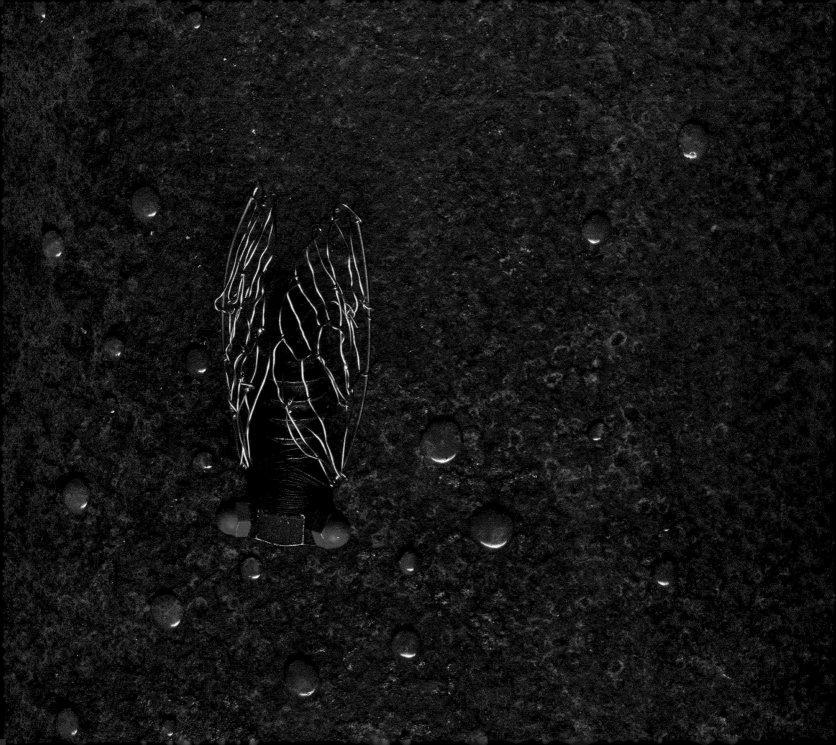

On the dewy trunk, step by step, a cicada gently picks his way.

Kyoshi

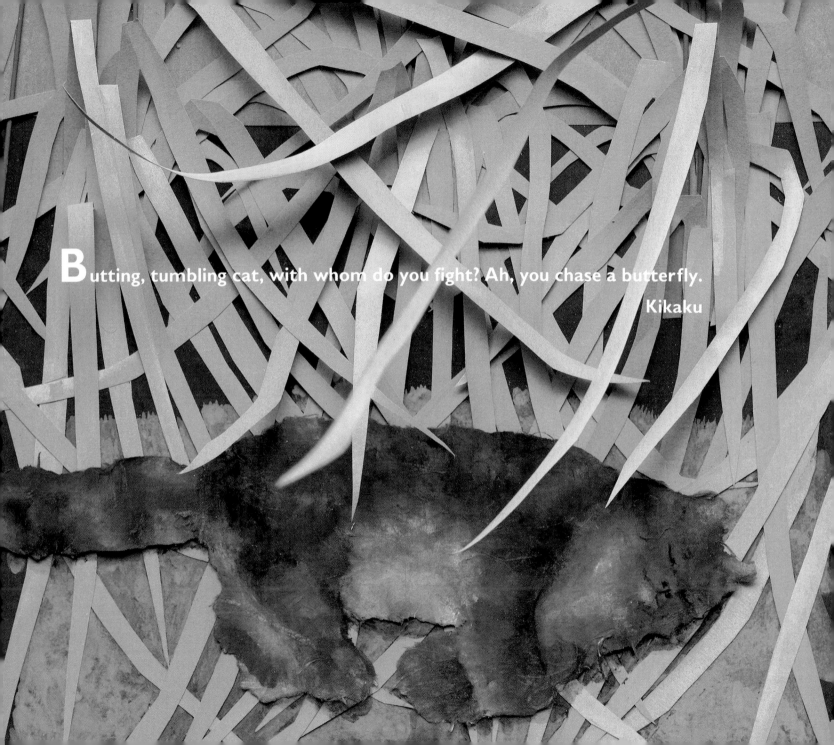

Butting, tumbling cat, with whom do you fight? Ah, you chase a butterfly.

Kikaku

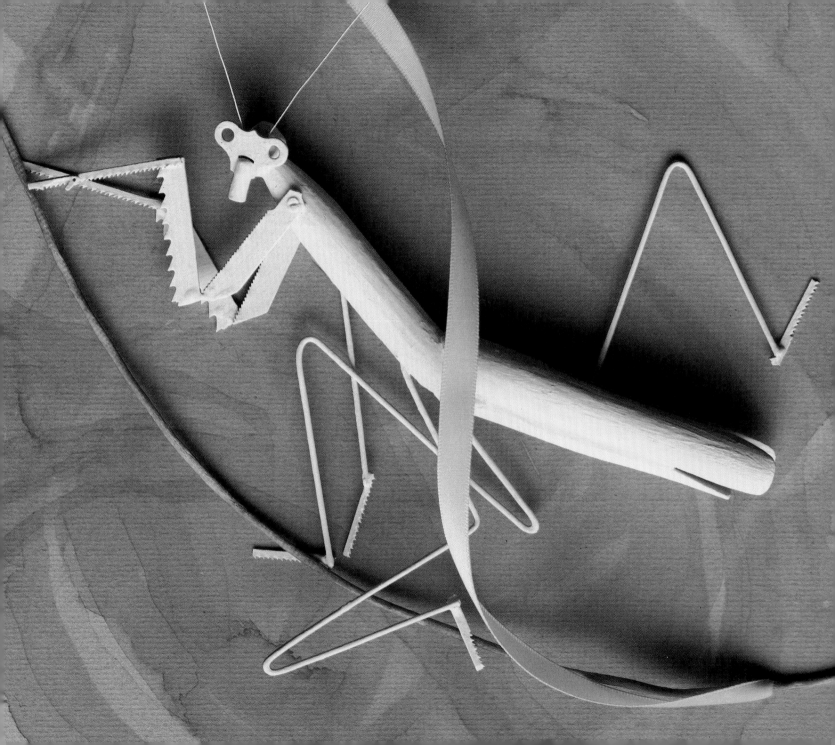

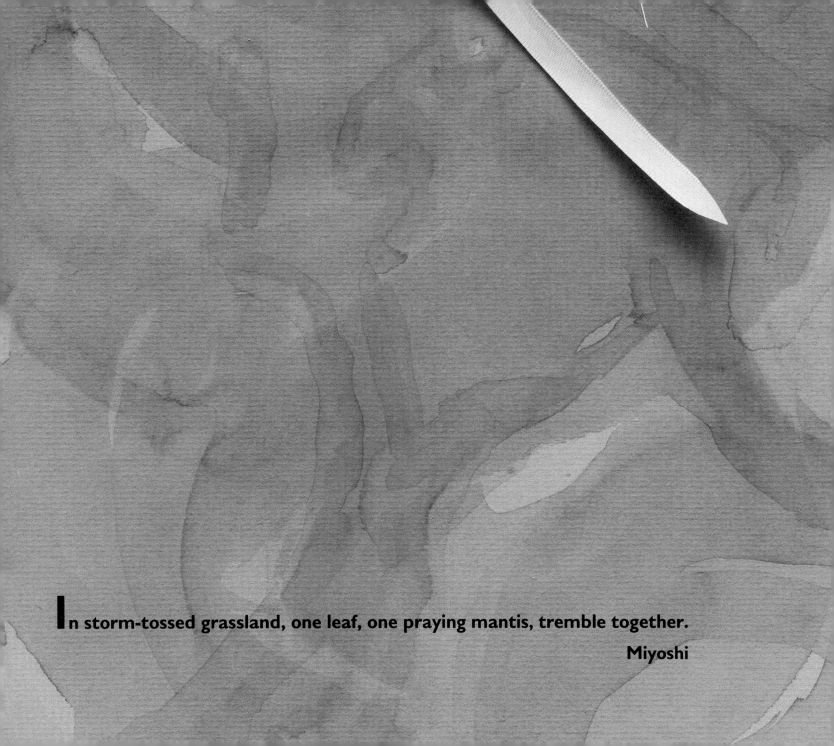

In storm-tossed grassland, one leaf, one praying mantis, tremble together.

Miyoshi

Oh, don't strike the fly! See? With knees bent and hands clasped he prays for his life.

Issa

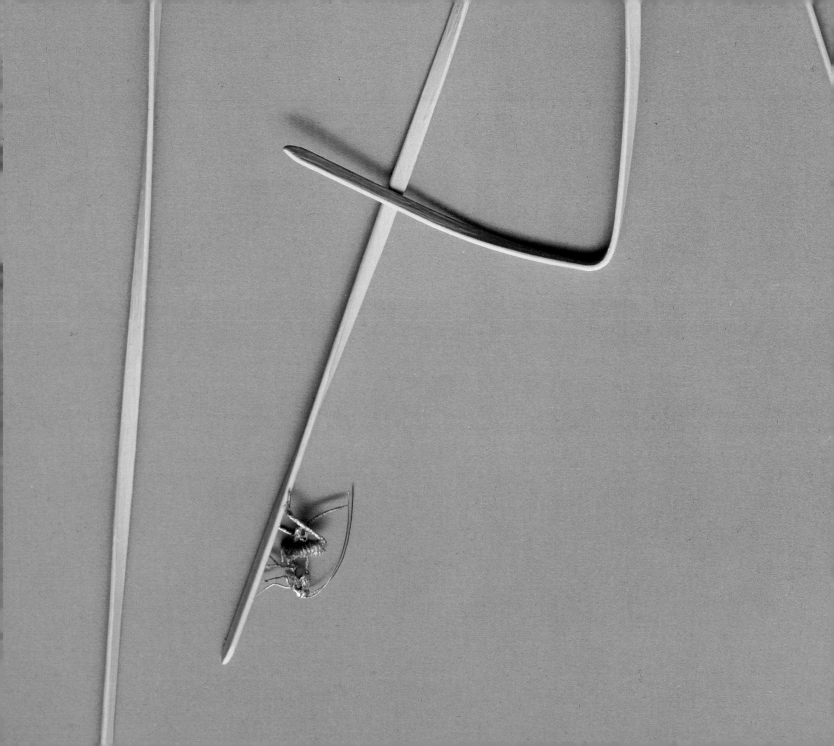

Above the chorus, listen! A single cricket shakes a golden bell.

Kyoshi

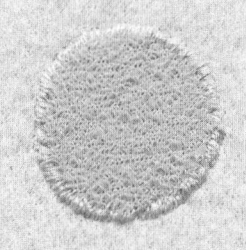

High noon! A hot sun bathes the town in quiet and stirs the sleeping dog.

Hajime

All at once, the storm! Overcome, a poor sparrow grasps a blade of grass.

Buson

Now the pond is still, and scattered water striders reunite at last.

Aohōzuki

Translators' Note

Haiku (pronounced high-koo) is a form of poetry that originated in Japan some seven hundred years ago. Unlike much of the poetry we are familiar with, haiku does not depend on rhyme or rhythm for its structure. Instead, nearly every haiku is composed of only seventeen syllables, divided into three units. The first unit contains five syllables, the second seven, and the last five again. Sometimes haiku is arranged as three separate lines, sometimes not.

The poems in this book are not exact translations of the original Japanese. For example, a literal translation of the verse on page 26 is "Sun beam striking place shifting/napping dog." The English version offered here adds details that enlarge upon the imagery without actually changing it.

It is best to read haiku very slowly. As you let each phrase add to the scene developing in your mind, a haiku will seem like a gem that breaks into hundreds of sparkling fragments of light when held against the sun.

Illustrator's Note

I wanted the pictures to have the same ease and playfulness as haiku, and the same spareness. Using pieces of ordinary life to make something special seemed appropriate. The materials are: #1: cookies, Elmer's glue, beads, tinfoil, dishtowel; #2: yam, potato and corn chips; #3: scissors, satin, velvet; #4: clamshell, crab legs, lobster claw, barnacle, gull feathers; #5: rock, buttons, cloth; #6: iron pipe, screw, capped hex nuts, copper wire, Stixall; #7: paper; #8: clothespins, clock key, coping saw and jigsaw blades, wire, ribbon; #9: seaglass, wire mesh, straw, screws, Scotch tape, thread; #10: skewers, wire, safety pins, screws, hairpins; #11: cloth, thread; #12: paper, beech and blueberry leaves, sesame seeds, Basmati rice; #13: chocolate-covered almonds, butterscotch-covered wire, gumdrops, wire metallic paper.

And of course the cat on page 19 is sleeping. I think she's dreaming of chasing a butterfly.